Reduce, Reuse, Recycle

Glass

Alexandra Fix

Heinemann
LIBRARY

www.heinemann.co.uk/library
Visit our website to find out more information about **Heinemann Library** books.

To order:

 Phone ++44 (0)1865 888066

 Send a fax to ++44 (0)1865 314091

 Visit the Heinemann Bookshop at www.heinemann.co.uk/library to browse our catalogue and order online.

First published in Great Britain by Heinemann Library, Halley Court, Jordan Hill, Oxford OX2 8EJ, part of Harcourt Education.
Heinemann is a registered trademark of Harcourt Education Ltd.

Editorial: Cassie Mayer and Diyan Leake
Design: Steven Mead and Debbie Oatley
Illustration: Jeff Edwards
Picture research: Ruth Blair
Production: Duncan Gilbert

Origination: Chroma Graphics (Overseas) Pte Ltd
Printed and bound in China by South China Printing Company Ltd

ISBN 978 0 431 90755 0
12 11 10 09 08

10 9 8 7 6 5 4 3 2 1

British Library Cataloguing in Publication Data
Fix, Alexandra, 1950-
  Glass. - (Reduce, reuse, recycle)
  1. Glass waste - Juvenile literature 2. Glass waste - Recycling - Juvenile literature 3. Waste minimization - Juvenile literature
  I. Title
  363.7'288

Acknowledgements
The publishers would like to thank the following for permission to reproduce photographs: Alamy pp. **4** (Gastrofotos), **5** (Ace Stock Limited), **6** (Foodfolio), **7** (Fstop2/Keith Pritchard), **10** (David Hoffman Photo Library), **11** (Robert Brook), **12** (Mark Boulton), **13** (Eddie Gerald), **16** (Matt Cardy), **17** (Tetra Images), **18** (Bob Purdue), **19** (Craig Holmes), **20** (Kim Karpeles), **23** (ImageState/Pictor International), **25** (Image100), **27**; Corbis pp. **8** (Kazuyoshi Nomachi), **9** (Sandro Vannini), **21** (Philip James Corwin), **24** (Erika Koch/Zefa); Ginny Stroud-Lewis pp. **15**, **26**; Science Photo Library pp. **14** (Martin Bond), **22** (Hank Morgan).

Cover photograph reproduced with permission of Corbis (Franc Enskat/zefa).

The publishers would like to thank Simon Miller for his assistance in the preparation of this book.

Every effort has been made to contact copyright holders of any material reproduced in this book. Any omissions will be rectified in subsequent printings if notice is given to the publishers.

Contents

Some words are shown in bold, **like this**. You can find out what they mean by looking in the glossary.

What is glass waste?

Glass is a strong, clear material that is used to make items such as windows, bottles, and containers. Glass is a useful material, but sometimes it is wasted.

↑ Food items are often stored in glass jars.

Glass waste ends up at **landfill sites** with other materials. ↑

Glass waste is glass that is thrown away. If glass is reused or **recycled**, it can be used over and over again.

What is made of glass?

Many foods and drinks are stored in glass bottles. Plates, cups, drinking glasses, and cookware are often made of glass. Pottery is sometimes **glazed** with a thin layer of glass.

↑ Food items such as vinegar are kept in glass bottles.

Boats can be made of fibreglass.
Fibreglass is a mixture of glass and plastic.

Small items such as light bulbs are made of glass. Large items such as windows, mirrors, and some doors are also made of glass.

Where does glass come from?

Glass is made from sand, soda ash, and lime. Sand comes from **dunes**, beaches, and the ocean floor. Lime is removed from limestone rock. Soda ash comes from a mineral rock called trona.

Sand is rock that has broken into tiny pieces over time.

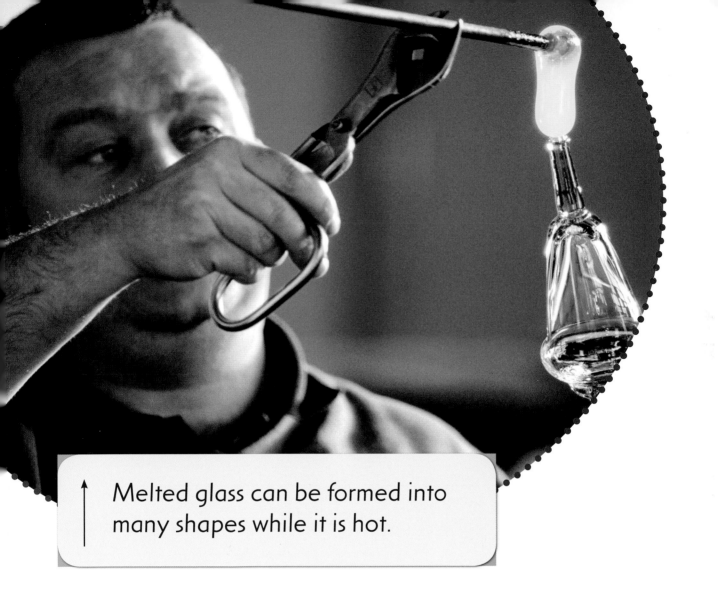

Melted glass can be formed into many shapes while it is hot.

Glass is made in **factories**. The sand, soda ash, and lime are melted and made into glass. **Fuels** such as coal, oil, or natural gas are used to heat the mixture.

Will we always have glass?

Sand is an important ingredient in making glass.

Sand, lime, and soda ash are **non-renewable resources**. Once these materials are used up, they will be gone forever.

10

We use other non-renewable resources as **fuels** to make glass. These include oil, coal, and natural gas. Every time we make new glass, we use up some of these fuels.

Glass **factories** can cause harmful air **pollution**.

What happens when we waste glass?

When glass is thrown away, it is taken to a **landfill site**. Tonnes of glass are buried in landfills. Glass bottles in a landfill could take up to a million years to rot away.

People throw away many tonnes of glass each year.
→

Bright sun shining through glass litter can start grass fires.

Glass **litter** is dangerous. People and animals can get cut by pieces of broken glass. Mosquitoes can lay their eggs in glass bottles and spread diseases.

13

How can we reduce glass waste?

The best way to reduce glass waste is to use less glass. Try not to buy glass items that you do not need. Ask your family to buy glass items that last a long time, such as energy-saving light bulbs.

Energy-saving light bulbs have to be replaced less often than normal light bulbs.

Many household glass bottles and jars can be **recycled**. ↑

Try not to buy drinks that come in glass bottles. Instead, reuse a drink container from home. You can fill it up at home with water or juice.

How can we reuse glass?

There are many ways to reuse glass. You can give unwanted glass items to charity shops. Other people might have a good use for your old mirrors, dishes, or drinking glasses.

Some companies mix used glass into concrete blocks.

A glass jar is handy for storing paintbrushes.

Think of new ways to reuse glass jars. One could hold a shell collection. Another could hold home-made biscuits. Decorate a glass jar to use as a vase.

How can we recycle glass?

When glass is **recycled**, it is melted down and used again to make a new item. Most **communities** have a recycling programme for glass, paper, and plastic.

Recycling bins are clearly labelled for cans, bottles, plastic, metal, and paper.

The only glass items that can be recycled from home are glass bottles and jars. After you have saved these items, rinse them out and remove any lids.

Only clear, brown, or green glass can be recycled.

Where can we take glass for recycling?

Some cities and towns have **recycling** collections. People can leave recycling bins outside their homes. A lorry picks up the items and takes them to a recycling centre.

Bins are left out for recycling lorries.

Some **communities** use fun ways to remind us to recycle glass.

You can also take used glass to a recycling centre or supermarket. From there, it is taken to a **factory**. Then it is made into recycled glass.

How is glass recycled?

After glass is taken to a **recycling** centre, it is sorted by colour. Then it is sent to a glass **factory**. There it is crushed into tiny pieces called cullet.

Crushed glass (cullet) is washed to remove glue and food particles.

Glass can be recycled over and over again.

Cullet is added to liquid glass in a **furnace**. The mixture is made into new glass objects.

How do we use recycled glass?

Recycled glass is safe to use for making new food and drink containers. Tiny glass pieces are used on sandpaper and for **sandblasting**.

Old glass bottles can be recycled to make new glass bottles.

At night, glass pieces in the paint make yellow lines look brighter.

Some finely crushed glass goes into **asphalt** for playgrounds and roads. It is also added to the paint used to draw the yellow lines on roads.

How can you take action?

You can help reduce glass waste. Ask friends and family to start **recycling** glass. You can help by washing out bottles and removing the lids.

Rinse bottles before putting them out for recycling.

Reduce

Reuse

Recycle

Your design here

LUCKY WINNERS
EACH WILL
WIN A
WASTE AWARE
ABERDEENSHIRE
GOODIE BAG

You can get take part in a project that helps reduce waste and **pollution**.

Ask a librarian to help you find your local recycling centre. Make a recycling poster to hang at school. By reducing glass waste, we can help keep our planet clean.

Make a bug jar

Ask an adult to help you with this project.

You can create your own bug jar by using an old glass container. Follow the steps below.

1. Put dirt, pebbles, twigs, and fresh leaves in a big glass jar.
2. Add a little moss or crumpled tissue paper to make a bug hiding place.
3. Put water in a small lid and set it in the jar.
4. Punch holes in the jar lid for air.

5. Catch or buy two crickets.

6. Feed the crickets bits of fruit, vegetables, green leaves, tropical fish flakes, or dry cat food.

You now have a bug jar! Check on your bug every day and write down what you see.

Fast facts

Most glass bottles and jars are made of some **recycled** glass.

The windows in cars are made of layers of glass and plastic. They will not break into sharp pieces.

Glass never wears out. It can be recycled forever.

Glossary

asphalt	mixture of sand, gravel, and tar used to make roads, car parks, and other hard surfaces
community	group of people who live in one area
dune	hill of sand found on coasts and in deserts
factory	building or buildings where something is made
fuel	material that is burned to create power or heat
furnace	closed-off space that is heated at high temperatures to warm a building or melt solid materials
glaze	cover with a thin layer of glass
landfill site	large area where rubbish is dumped, crushed, and covered with soil
litter	rubbish
non-renewable resource	material taken from the earth that cannot be replaced by nature
pollution	wastes and poisons in the air, water, or soil
recycle	break down a material and use it again to make a new product. Recycling is the act of breaking down a material and using it again.
sandblasting	cleaning a surface with sand and tiny pieces of glass that are pushed by a strong blast of air

Find out more

Books to Read

Materials: Glass, Chris Oxlade (Heinemann Library, 2002)

Using Materials: How We Use Glass, Chris Oxlade (Raintree, 2005)

Why Should I Recycle? Jen Green (Hodder Wayland, 2002).

Websites

Waste Watch work to teach people about reducing, reusing, and recycling waste. You can visit www.recyclezone.org.uk to find out more information about waste and to try some online activities..

Find out where you can recycle in your local area at: www.recyclenow.com by typing in your postcode. You can also find out more about which items can be recycled, more facts about waste, and what you can do to help!

Index